Juniper

Yvonne Beaudry

© 2025 Yvonne Beaudry

All rights reserved. This book or parts thereof may not be reproduced in any form, stored in any retrieval system, or transmitted in any form by any means—electronic, mechanical, photocopy, recording, or otherwise—without prior written permission of the publisher, except as provided by United States of America copyright law and fair use. For permission requests, contact the publisher at the email address below.

beaudrypoetry@gmail.com

ISBN: 979-8-9928130-0-5 (paperback)

ISBN: 979-8-2891334-8-9 (paperback)

ISBN: 979-8-9928130-1-2 (eBook)

Cover art by Rachel Beaudry.

Visit the author's website at beaudrypoetry.com

Acknowledgements

After years of writing poetry in private, I can't believe my poetry has the chance to see the light of day. So many people have played a part in making my dream a reality. I want to start by saying a huge thank you to Amanda Meli.

Amanda, you are my #1 cheerleader and there is no way I could have made it this far without you. I appreciate all the car rides and conversations in your car. I mean, it's what kept this project alive and breathing after all.

Thank you, Rachel Beaudry, for the cover art and feedback. I fell in love with the cover as soon as you sent me the finished product. I also want to thank you for putting up with all my inexperience when it comes to art.

Sharon Meli, there's a conversation that I had with you that changed my perspective and ignited some sort of determination within me. I felt things shift and I felt more committed to publishing my poetry after that. I am so grateful for your words, your feedback, and your support.

I know I'm going on a bit of a limb here, but I want to thank the people who encouraged me to write poetry—before I even considered putting together a collection. Thank you: Linda Wasiak, Arielle Wasiak, Miriam Sas (a.k.a. Ms. Kranz), Hannah Nale, Jeremy Maldonado, Tiffany Arnold, and last but never least Emily Ngo.

Of course, I can't forget my family. I want to thank my parents and my sisters for their love and support. I love you guys, and I would never trade you for another family. I appreciate my family members who came to see me read at open mics, and the ones who wanted to go, but were never able to make it.

Lastly, I want to thank everyone who has given me direct and indirect feedback, especially my proofreaders. I'm sure that there are some people that have helped me more than they realize.

To all those who are finding

their place in the world.

Table of Contents

Desert Flame Daylily 1

Deep Brown Eyes 2

Black and Blue Ballerina 3

Keeping Up Appearances 4

Snow Queen 5

Bonnie 7

Two Seconds 8

Her Voice 10

My Not-So-Little Bracelet 11

Machismo 12

A Lesbian is Not a Lesbian 13

Pink Boys 14

"Raphael, Hold Your Fire" 15

Blood is Red 16

Marigolds Are Forever Ruined 17

Dead (Girl)Friend 18

Black Licorice Tongue Behind Golden Teeth 20

Grey Goodbye 21

Ethnic Exile 22

Pretty People 23

Claustrophobic 24

Photographs Are Time Machines Anyone Can Make 25

Living with a Stranger 26

Violeta 27

The Boy Was Candy 28

Blue Thread of the Sea 29

Waiting 30

King of the Slugs 31

Angel Baby 32

The Truth About Ticks 33

Car Ride with Amanda 35

Robin-Breast Bones 36

Magazine Smiles 37

Less is More 38

Valarie: The Mustard Seed 39

Child of God 40

Screwing a Goddess 41

She is Devil 42

Saved by Skylarks 43

Sam 44

Growing Up Costs a Ruby 45

Memento Mori 46

The Last Year to Spare 47

Convalescence 48

Eli's Lingering Embers 49

Ghost Man Blues 50

Origami Horse 51

Juniper

Desert Flame Daylily

She wanders through fragmented minds
as a delicate ring of fire, always expanding
until she becomes invisible. Her eyes glisten
like supernova stardust and her voice is pink sleep.
A girlish smile graces her lips every time she stretches too far,
spilling her colors out of the lines of time
until they bleed from the past into the present.

Deep Brown Eyes

Because of her, I fell in love
with deep brown eyes that pull a person in,
like a stellar black hole collapsing in on itself.

An enticing darkness that draws a person in
spinning them round and round,
in a game of pin the tail
on whatever you can find in the vastness.

Just two seconds of eye contact,
and an overwhelming heat erupts
from the flock of sparrows
sandwiched between a pupil and sclera.

The wrinkles of chaos are smoothed out
by a gentle buzz of walnut, as the heat
gives way to a syrupy warmth: melted caramel.

Brown eyes feel like home,
a safe place to hide
from the blizzard of lies
outside. The cinnamon glow
is bright enough to steal the light from stars.

Black and Blue Ballerina

Blue blue ballerina
shuffling silently across the arena,
the whirling little asteroid
falters from the sharp prick of her thyroid.

She begs her body for a day of gray,
a compromise she doesn't trust to stay.
Still, in desperation she makes the plea,
for her mother's sake she needs to be free.

While lights from above subdue her vision
her mind's eye grants her a lucid prevision;
one day her bones will no longer be white.
The reality of black begins to bite

but she remains a dancer.
And yet, her mother tells her
she has black black cancer.

There must be another answer.

Keeping Up Appearances

A thousand butterflies
flutter in my mouth,
poking holes in my tongue,
smearing feces on my teeth.
My lips are sealed.

The fractionated membrane within
will soon create an exit in my lips.
Desperately, I clamp them shut.
Wings batter against my gums—
transforming them into a brown-green sewer.

The sweet smell of flowers in my veins
is what attracted them in the first place.
Once inside, there was no escape.
I swallow spurts of blood
and the guts of butterflies.

Their dark limbs peek out
between my teeth, any time I grin.
Because of this, I've learned to grimace,
as my tongue sweeps away any evidence.

No one dares to question a lemon that's sour.

Snow Queen

Blades of ice snake around her forearms
in solid sleeves that pull her into the frigid unknown.
"A life for a life" was the deal she had agreed to—
not knowing how those words could twist.

Before she could take her next breath,
her heart froze, into a dark, sticky popsicle.
The sickled muscle has begun to reek
with a bitter mahogany meanness.

And now, her life belongs to the winter wind.

Walking the streets,
she is surrounded by warm hands
and worm hearts, and does what she must
to blur into the background.

Carefully, she breathes on each word
before she dares to speak,
terrified of becoming a firebird
that burns down the kingdom.

It is only a hollow attempt to defrost
the ice shield placed over her smile.

Her eyes are pale pink in the light
like the opaque print of a pearl,
nothing goes through them:
neither in nor out.

Every night she lies in bed
kissing fire, to burn
her white-gold dreams
into lingering cinders.

Fantasies of death
have become a thrilling secret,
that she buries in the graveyard
of her heart—filling up each plot.

Reality stings with every frosted exhale,
and only gets worse when she finds the life
she gave everything up to save.

All she can see is the crystallized fear,
as the familiar fondness drains
from her princess's eyes. Her only wish
is that she said goodbye to begin with.

Bonnie

Silent fear lingers
in the tips of her fingers.
She shrinks her spine
until she is compressed,
like a beetle made from origami.

She believes being invisible
is her secret superpower:
as if she can fool monsters
when she is a white magnolia
hanging from a thick black cord.

She bleeds all over the concrete
from the stab of their talons and fangs.
She plucks out each one, holds it close,
closes her eyes and makes a wish—
hoping that she can make less of a mess.

She tries to disappear,
but reality runs rampant
as the monsters sniff her out at each turn.
Still, the ivory glass of her heart,
it glitters like the Mississippi moon
against a sky of obsidian clouds.

Two Seconds

Bittersweet chocolate
liquifies his thoughts.
Eyes sprint. Panting, puffing
playing tag in between cash registers.

His thoughts collide
with the astonishment of being tagged. Oxygen
tumbles haphazardly out of his mouth.

Clip-clopping vibrations hum
within his heart, echoing simultaneously
through all four chambers.

Ribs screech, shriek, and snap,
violently severing his spine.
Exposed.

Groaning lungs struggle
to destroy the paralysis.
Two seconds of stillness,
so silent he questions his vitality.

Incoherent sounds masquerading
as syllables, fruitlessly smite his teeth.
Trying to escape is like sweeping the desert.

Click.
"Cerebral function activated."
Unexceptional, Typical, and Trite

return home to an unaccommodating landlord.
For two seconds he was free.

Two seconds.

Her Voice

cuts through as cleanly as a disinfected scalpel.
There is a certain clarity to it
that overshadows anything a gem has to offer.
It tilts and bends like a skilled tightrope walker
carelessly toying with the audience.

Each word is granted an equal opportunity
to reach its intended target,
as it cartwheels through her lips.
The detached friendliness
makes it all-the-more inviting.

There is never an expectation
as the words march out
in a line that is so straight and neat
(it actually sparks the interest of some addicts.)

Behind her words, there are tiny pouches
of powdered poison. No matter how
sacred and holy, angels too must fight.

Deep in the throes of war, her voice is a beacon
attracting all creatures,
like lost flies drawn to artificial light.

My Not-So-Little Bracelet

The clock on the desk is somehow numb,
lagging on the image 11:13. Night and day
the numbers appear. Rooting through my bracelets,
my hand gets tangled with a string
of green pastel-pez-pieced owls.

There is an urge to chew each plastic charm
until the dust is lost under my tongue,
clinging like unwanted pieces of glitter.
The carnal craving: a love letter.

That overstretched bracelet weeps
in an unhinged display
of raw affection and curiosity,
which drowns out the sound of my thoughts.
Maybe I'm the one who struggles to adjust…

or perhaps I've adjusted too much.
Remnants of an untimely demise
stalk every aspect of my life—
leaving nothing but haunted memories
that roam around (mostly under the radar).

Machismo

A Puerto Rican flag blinks at me
behind a fog of fear and frustration.
My body is pinned in place, like a perfect
updo—drenched in expensive hairspray.
Meanwhile, cans of "Axe" line up across the way.

The facade of the perfect man.

Grey floor, grey beds, white walls, and a
white ceiling. My sky-blue basketball shorts
(thin as a toothpick) contain the only color I see.
As his body presses behind me,
my body is mistaken for wet cement
that begs to be imprinted.

He thinks he is subtle.
He thinks he is clever.
But my body, well, it knows better.

A Lesbian is Not a Lesbian

I have been training for this position since birth.
An attraction to women as a woman
is the sole requirement and is ingrained in my being
like the stitches on a baseball.
Despite this, I'm considered a wretched outlier.
I don't understand how definitions can be warped
by the voluntary addition of fictitious mutations.

The loss of reality permeates my blood-brain barrier.
Confusion lays sickly fragile eggs within my consciousness.
Each one shivers like a much-too-full water balloon.
For intelligent beings, humans are embarrassingly stupid.
We imitate our surroundings, mindlessly searching
for validation with the hope of earning a moment of belonging.

Humans need labels and words to guide them.
Nothing seems to be comprehended without language.
But, too many words are being used
blurring lines like a bleeding rainbow.

The danger lies in the disguise.
Inclusion has become an erasure.
Bigotry lurks beneath the surface of acceptance.
I have no choice, I cannot silently accept
the elimination of my identity.

For as long as the rainbow bleeds
I cannot exist—not in the way I used to.

Pink Boys

Softer than a baby's grasp,
these boys are the wings
floating above the night-time breeze.

Their chests are constructed
from the petals of carnations
and shoot out torpedoes of laughter.

They ride on stallions of steel,
making their rounds
as they inspect the environment,

searching for the suffering.
Without fail, they cry—
heavy drops in the silence—over what is found.

They never turn away—not even to hide their eyes.

"Raphael, Hold Your Fire"

He feigns ignorance
as his eyelids stutter.
"Raphael, hold your fire."
Rage is only temporary,
but, blinds permanently.

His dreams have been
lobotomized, as they tank
to the sandy depths of his mind.
"Raphael, hold your fire."
Dreams are only remixed memories.

Air moves the flames
as they fan out before it is time.
"Raphael, hold your fire."
There can be no cure
if there is no disease.

Strips of topaz lightning
burst forth from a miniature bottle,
shooting out in an arrow arc—
quicker than the light of infinity.

Raphael never could hold his fire.

Blood is Red

Outside her window,
false allies crawl through the blackness.
Shiny white fangs gleam
in the spaces between starlight.

Everyone outside
looks like a vampire to her.
They don't bleed.
Not in the way she does.

The red fangs close in on her
closely followed by the red eyes.
She desperately drains every ounce of red
from her own body in sheer disgust.

Her fingers burn from live wires:
from playing where she shouldn't.
Tainted eyes stare back at her through the glass.
Lemon-yellow eyes are marred
with blood-red flecks from far below.

The bones splinter in her fists
like rotted wood, as she blurs the lines
between yellow and red, creating
a burst of tangerine that stains her smile.

Marigolds Are Forever Ruined

Fat drops of avarice drip down
from the clouds above. The silence
of the streets drills into hearts
like burrowing dung beetles.

Stray segments of the sky burn
from the charcoal tears of violence.
The pollution chokes on its own
desperate attempt at self-defense.

Carnelian eyes gaze into an empty horizon,
as impurities smudge the marigold smiles
that once resided in the valley of peace.

Dead (Girl)Friend

She was the untethering of attraction,
with dark, cavernous eyes and ravenous features.
Vampire fangs slid out from behind her lips
like the smooth creep of an earthworm.

Whenever she spoke to me,
I could smell the butterflies on her breath
from all the dreams she had swallowed.
More accurately, it was the cluster of preludes
where both of our dreams intersected.

Her presence was elusive
and the space without her was eerie.
Like a rebellious teen, she would sneak out
the second my eyes would shut.
Two feet in and two feet out
seemed to be her way of life.

Her mind was all black haze and pink steps.
The many rooms of her mind
united me with the human experience.
There were hidden vaults
with freshwater pearls and the promise
of treasure had me transfixed.
Obsessively, I needed more.

Overstimulation clouded my conscience
as I slit her throat with naïve fondness,
staining my hands with crimson regret.

Later, she revealed that she was cut
from the same cloth as Lazarus.
Without a back glance, she got up
like a deer struck by a car and walked away.

Only I know I got away with murder,
but we both know her body will never be found.

Black Licorice Tongue Behind Golden Teeth

Carefully undoing the bows of ribbon from rusty branches,
he cradles an abandoned home with violent hands.
The stains of spilled blood last forever
and he knows that truth with every fiber of his being. Softly
the broken twigs spill over the sides of his hands
like an emptying anthill. Despite his efforts
to right past wrongs, he cannot escape
the consequences of his fate.

Grey Goodbye

I saw the world in monochrome on the day she said goodbye.
It wasn't charcoal grey or heather grey,
but the kind of grey that fills your stomach like a broken
    bicycle pump.
The kind of grey that blots out any scrap of color,
blurring the lines of time until every day is identical;
practically static, like a mouth filled to the brim
with previously chewed bubble gum. Teeth gripped in a lockup.

This pigment shreds memories into unrecognizable husks
of hollow loss, which morph into the mutated mistake of regret.
It can effortlessly cause anger to swell through too-thin pipes,
creating a tinny whistle as the veins of brains pop one
    after another.
Grey mush covers the inner walls of these skulls.

This elusive shade enjoys snagging onto hope and
    starry-eyed dreams,
transforming them into shaggy, ratty, moth-eaten curtains.
Motivation and passion succumb to grey persuasion,
the same kind that was hidden in her whispered goodbye.

Ethnic Exile

The notion of belonging makes her smile.
She is torn between the two halves that make her whole
and the skeleton of her identity crumbles in a pile.

With one deep breath, she stomachs the bile—
the result of fearing half of her soul.
The notion of belonging makes her smile.

She alternately favors each half with a flimsy dial
and eventually, the instability takes its toll.
The skeleton of her identity crumbles in a pile.

The desire for validation created this exile
and it all began when she surrendered her control.
The notion of belonging makes her smile.

The expectations of society taste vile
on the back of her throat, leaving a hole
in the skeleton of her identity—so it crumbles in a pile.

Each piece of her racial profile is categorized by file
and seems impossible to combine into one singular bowl.
Still, the notion of belonging makes her smile.
But, the skeleton of her identity—it crumbles in a pile.

Pretty People

Pretty people don't tell lies
instead, they hide with their eyes.
Straight edges and a symphony
of symmetry shield them from misery.

Pretty people don't sob and wail,
their skin never turns pale.
Tears are shed in a delicate way
like a rose petal floating along the bay.

Pretty people don't feel pain
when all they seem to do is gain
foothold after foothold.
The ground beneath is never cold.

Pretty people don't fall in love,
taking out time to dispose of
any ripening imperfections,
trading freckles for infections.

Pretty people don't exist—
not like they do in this list.
Ugliness lives inside of us all
preparing us for our fated fall.

Claustrophobic

Small house with a blue roof and her need to please
cram within nine square feet. The smell of exertion consumes
fresh air like bonbons from a box. Feeble fabric does little to
protect her purity as the feel of his hands leaves stains no one
understands. The grass in the distance blurs into one green goblin
when she fears there is no escape from the hands that press her
clothes into her skin. Standing still like a streetlight in winter,
she thinks to herself: "The game is almost over."
Her pants are bunched and an invisible rash forms from his
cheap imitation of a wave eroding the shore.

Photographs Are Time Machines Anyone Can Make

Within the borders of a photo,
she sees the picture of perfection.
Her mother's smile—a memory
that pulls her like a tourist trap.
She feels the collapse
of her heart as she sinks
to the floor. The recap
kidnaps her mind. Trapped.

Rifling through snapshots of the past
is a firetrap, and the image of her mother's smile
is the match igniting the demonic flame—
the one that burns the edges of heaven.
She quickly swallows the slab of guilt
before it becomes swollen
and suffocates her—
an all too familiar feeling.

Her last prayer burns
into the remnants of muted truths
and nostalgic safety nets.
She always forgets, that in the end,
a photograph can only go so far.

Living with a Stranger

There's a stranger in her house.
His words stick to her like cinnamon glue.
Well, at least he's a good spouse.

Every day she feels like a louse;
she doesn't think he even has a clue.
There's a stranger in her house.

Between his eyes, she flees like a mouse
avoiding the crush of his shoe.
Well, at least he's a good spouse.

The world creates love to douse
him in a burdening red hue.
There's a stranger in her house.

He never grips at the front of her blouse.
He was near her but not with her, as she grew.
Well, at least he's a good spouse.

She thinks he used to be her lighthouse
guiding her through the blue.
Now, there's a stranger in her house.
Still, he's always been a good spouse.

Violeta

Abstract swirls of red and blue
both paint the inside of my veins.
To the naked eye, the red is absent
while blue flows freely out of every pore.

Violent streaks of violet
collide in my field of vision,
creating a blended film
that saturates the world around me.

On the surface, my words
are tainted in blue-tinted varnish.
At the heart of every syllable
is a speck of raging red.

It was never my intention
to pass as a bluebell,
when I am a stalk of lavender.
I guess the red pieces
just got lost in the blue.

The Boy Was Candy.

His eyes swirled like cotton candy
with the contrasting colors of saltwater taffy.
His smile hid like a packet of pop rocks,
waiting to spring the surprise within.
His nose was a ruthless lemon warhead
that became sweet over the years.
His love was a bottomless triple-berry trifle,
plenty to share with the world around him.

No surface remained untouched on the day,
on the day his life broke wide open—
like a crashing jar of maraschino cherries.

Blue Thread of the Sea

A blue thread
with the blackness
of the bottom of the ocean

connects us at the edge
of forgiveness and hope.
Patience runs thin at the frayed ends.

Frightened eyes leak into that thread,
inviting the cracks in our smiles
to be the blackest of blues.

We are exhausted
from carrying each other's weight,
but it's not our fault we can't forget.

Instead, we collect fondness,
like mini riptides
that drag against each of our ribcages
in the middle of the night.

Waiting

Little buds of ice sprout up from the soil of her flesh,
watered by the frigid channels of her veins.
She shrink-wraps her soul to keep warm.
Sitting still in the frost will kill her.

Her thighs are melded to the floor,
while gnats pick at the fuzz on her face.
She watches the dust
as it floats past her eyelashes.

Nothing motivates and she looks like a lunatic
chewing at the bars of her self-made cell.
The only way to escape is through the door.
It is wide open, welcoming her with its warmth.

Instead of using the door of possibilities,
she has been using the sawdust and icicles
found in the freezer to shape her destiny.

With her cramped heart in one hand
and a fistful of hair in the other,
she waits.

She patiently watches the exit shrink
as her body freezes and her eyes droop down,
replaying the last decision that she will ever make.

King of the Slugs

Foolishly, she believed she had a chance
to heal and to forget, but the trance
around her remains a challenge to reverse.
She has been given a king's curse.

Hopelessly, she begs for permission to sin,
anything to avoid taking it on the chin.
Confused as to whether this is a lesson
or a mistakenly overlooked mission.

Still, his name slips from her tongue,
like a lone penny carelessly flung
onto the floor below as it rolls
through cracks and hidden holes.

His smile grips her veins
like the clutch of a nearly missed train.
Sloppy hairline fractures line
her wrists from the pressure of his design.

His stubby slug fingers squirm,
inching along always hungry for harm.
Relishing in the slightest bit of contact
his presence has never been compact.

Her skin rots from the slime of the slugs
as he enters with ease on a throne of bugs.
She would give anything to make the curse end
but she is only a puppet and too old to play pretend.

Angel Baby

Angel Baby keep my secrets near.
I promise you will not forget the sound
of my pain creeping up each ear,
and my words will wrap around
any attempt you make at healing—
burying you completely in the feeling.

Angel Baby fight by my side.
I never wanted you to be alone
but in hindsight, I may have lied.
There was so much I hadn't known
when the gentle tilt of your voice began to burn.
Still, I expected you to always return.

Angel Baby with your shield of light
travel by my side at night.
Be my barrier down this broken path,
as I bathe my body and laugh
in the glow of your evergreen eyes—
knowing it is impossible to tell you lies.

The Truth About Ticks

A little boy squirms and shifts in his seat
as tweezers approach his shoulder—
a frenzied dance of twitches and pings of metal.

His father wields the tiny metal appendage
and the boy knows everything will be okay.
Still, the metallic prodding triggers some doubt.

"What happens if the head comes off?"
The boy has heard the cautions of losing
the head of a tick while extracting it.

"I've done this plenty of times
and that has never happened.
Don't worry about it."

Eyes fixated on the magic metal wand,
he holds his breath while his dad pinches.
The fluidity is like a temporary respirator for the boy.

A peculiar black dot niggles where the tick once was.
A shriek pierces the kitchen walls.
Seized by fear, the boy's head is now a bucking bronco.

The father soothes him with gentle promises
and beautiful lies since the truth is unknown.
Still, fathers always know best.

Later that night, the boy is roused from his sleep.
He feels it before he can open his eyes.
A vibration sounds throughout his arm

with his shoulder being the epicenter.
The sensation is as constant as the tolling
of church bells on Sunday morning.

A dreadful rumble cascades down his arm
as his veins bend to and fro,
like little pipe-cleaner soldiers.

His skin bumps up in a three-dimensional rhythm
of alternating sides. The movement within
his arm is frantic and desperate.

Something is trying to burst through his skin
in a violent wave of effort. Closing his eyes,
he lets go, finding the truth in the lies—
the ones his dad hid behind.

Car Ride with Amanda

Sitting next to her as she drives
(homemade hummus bumping my feet)
my heart heats up as it beats harder.

With sunglasses shielding her eyes from the world
and a leopard bra spilling out the side of her black tank top
she chews on a potato chip.
"I was craving salt."

A familiar song leaks from the worn-out speakers
and her voice sways rhythmically, inspired by the soul of the Earth.
Struck by awe, my composure slips and I am unaware
of my face glitching into a smile as I turn to her—
studying the many versions of her heart.

Robin-Breast Bones

Fever paints my bones in scarlet oil,
as medication in the form of repentance
promises a bleaching remedy:
erase the past with a front of falsities.

My thoughts are controlled by this sickness,
I hear it calling to me in my sleep.
It needs my help to survive, but,
maybe I don't want to get better.

I've lived with it for so long
it has become a friendly neighbor;
one that I feel protective toward.
I refuse to kill the parasite, instead

I deflect the blame elsewhere and accept the pain.
I would rather treat this illness like a blessing
and not the accident it is known to be.

But my bones resemble the breasts of robins and that
abnormality cannot be ignored.
I must be dying and maybe the disease is to blame.
Maybe I should accept the bone-bleaching ritual.

Frail white bones are better than strong red bones.
Superficial cover-up is better than genuine healing.
Fraudulence is better than authenticity.
I'll feel better once I'm like everyone else;
stripped of my color—just like everyone else.

Magazine Smiles

The women in the magazine
spring out smiles of citrus
in daffodil yellow, that on occasion bleed.
The taste is sour on their tongues.

The women wear their cracked
and chalky smiles with pride;
their faces elongated with fear—
a hint at how small they really are.

Always afraid that the end is near,
their smiles are created from torn flesh
and manufactured joy.

They don't last for more than one second—
not when they're all too tired
from holding onto something far from real.

Less is More

Her common sense cowers in the corner,
spending whatever scraps of energy it has left
on the act of forgetting.

If she stops eating, then she will stop feeling.

Rage-driven rumbling begins to gurgle
in fitful bursts. She smiles as the intensity deepens.
Agony sounds out from deep within
but is lost in the swell of the changing tides.

Painful pangs croak out in her brain,
begging for mercy, but a dense, soundproof blanket
covers the surrounding area.

The fat disintegrates, as her name is forgotten.

She has less of a body, but no more of a smile
than she did before. She doesn't understand.
She has less of a body, but more pain to hide
than she did before. She doesn't understand.

Her dreams of fulfillment are ashen
as they fall over her barren body:
burying her and her misguided attempt to control.

Valarie: The Mustard Seed

Scars paint her body in a tapestry
of lessons and memories, the images
blur and sting like hawks pecking at her face—
turning her lips a metallic maroon.

Bronze armor covers her body
to conceal the rust of neglect on her ribcage.
The bones jut out from the pressure
but the bleeding has always given her pleasure.

Her heart is dried out and shriveled,
from soaking in the saltwater
that collects behind her lacrimal dam.

Every day she roams her lonely town,
searching for a freshwater river
to pump her heart back up to size.

There is one reason she keeps
the crimson raisin around.

She smiles down at the mustard seed,
hidden away from the rest of the world
in the deep creases of her palm.
Her very own Hail Mary.

Child of God

The eyes of God hid behind hers
as isolated identities became interlaced.
Her patchwork love colored in the cracks of her irises
in a kaleidoscope of moral consequence.

Upon closer inspection, the guise of her eyes
decayed and revealed dried flecks of debris splattered
within the reflection of her pupils. The remnants
of a silent but brutal battle within her brain.
An innocent friendship nearly triggered a faith fatality.

Sacred confessions sprang within a secret sanctum,
as noiseless chatter surrounded the intimate
and impenetrable bubble, that was created
from the air of classrooms and hallways.
No decree of exile ever peeled itself from the mold of her lips.

Staring into the soul of sin incarnate, she would smile;
the hope born from that action was anything but juvenile.

Screwing a Goddess

Bright notes of sorrow ring out,
ricocheting off the streaked glass
and stained leaf water of a decayed city.
Distracting herself, she collects the palladium plates
that poke out of the debris lying by her feet.

Sweet, minty eyes meet hers
and half a laugh gets stuck in her teeth from her luck.
She can read the telltale signs like a calling card.
Electricity pulses through her veins
drumming out a steady beat— with eyes on Iris.

With human hands, she grips a body made of
Plutonian bends and dreams that will never come true.
Sugar kisses flutter against her cheeks,
doing nothing to stop the rotting firmament
she so desperately wants to forget.

She hungrily kisses the gentle lips of Iris,
and almost loses herself in the soft clouds of warmth.
But as she pulls back, the silver blindness of moonlight
reflects from the calloused lips she just touched.
The remaining winter-mint eyes bore into her
and the panic settles in her stomach with a drop.

She is Devil

A chopped-up face stares back at me,
with botched blue eyes that blur
every time the full moon appears.

Hellish pride paints an off-center smile
on the ghastly face facing me without opposition.
Boundaries crack before me as I become nothing.

A splintered crucifix punctures my side
every time I turn to hide.
Nothing exists—but those blue eyes…

Some nights, I see the devil slowly crawl
out from behind blue rubble.
I can't find God…I'm in trouble.

Saved by Skylarks

In a corner of darkness, a man
looms over an effervescent doll,
plucking the tender treasure
from the scalding bath. Meanwhile,
shelved dolls scream silently in the background.

Another unexpected addition
to improve his growing collection.
With a twitch of his fingers, the doll droops
in a subtle attempt to create distance.
Reflexively, he pins the wooden arms in place
and artificial eyes seem to widen. Too subtle
to even register, so he continues
while the blurred blinks begin.

The manufactured mouth
folds in on itself as human hands wander.
Greedily, his canines sink seamlessly
into the whorls and indents of wooden flesh,
consuming the elusive healing energy within.
Virtues snag on his teeth, getting wedged
in between molars. He yanks them out
thoughtlessly, with a grime-filled pinky nail.

Immobile and scraped hollow,
the rawness robs the doll's eyes of their shine
and the fading begins. First in the eyes,
next in the mind, but the serenade of several skylarks
from the crowded shelf above
acts as a cellophane for the brain.

Newfound purpose calcifies the doll's boiled bones
when a wooden warble interrupts the prayerful silence of the night.

Sam

He has an invisible immunity
to superficial charms and lucky pearls.
His hands have been carved
by soft whale teeth and hollow shame.

Embarrassment sticks to the heat of his feet,
as a lingering reminder to block out the noise.
One by one, he peels away the scars
and he is beautiful. He always was.

Sometimes he runs away,
but his smile is lovely—
dusting off his burnt bones.
His eyes wisp away

in silent muddy waters,
but his laugh is freshly scooped
ice cream—melting far too fast.
An idiot in the daylight

but a genius in the moonlight.
He's the unassuming breeze
within the stillness, in the middle
of a hazy summer afternoon.

Growing Up Costs a Ruby

"Nothing's gonna hurt you, baby."
She looks into her mother's eyes,
and is face-to-face with a dying ruby.

Two years later and she has grown chubby,
her peers hurl insults while she cries.
"Nothing's gonna hurt you, baby."

She believes the words, she thinks, maybe.
She knows all her mother's lies,
and is face-to-face with a dying ruby.

Time has made her mother's voice crabby
chipping away at her credibility, what a surprise:
"Nothing's gonna hurt you, baby."

The new friends she has found make her snobby,
pressuring her to grow up and sever familial ties,
but she is face-to-face with a dying ruby.

She wonders what it would be like to be free,
but freedom comes at a cost and she quietly sighs
when she is face-to-face with a dying ruby.
"Nothing's gonna hurt you, baby."

Memento Mori

The essence of its beauty
is amplified by her unbalanced tears,
leaving its music untouched and unmarred
by horrid human hands.
Abandonment is a radioactive kindness
that swims in the shallows of success.

Only half a decade passes, before the resentment
meets her half a mile from the hollow body of her long-lost love.
The bitterness boils within and she burns
from the past—like thousands of witches before—
the moment her fingers graze the smooth neck of wood.

The envy seeps under her skin
from the unscarred body and innocence
that taunts her, as she savagely crushes
the tiniest fragments of hope within her soul.
Unaware, the instrument continues to collect dust

on its bow, forgotten and ready to let go;
ready to forgive the neglect and move on,
accepting the fate of extinction.
The time has now come for her to let go,
but she is not ready yet
and instead, spends her nights denying that she is next.

The Last Year to Spare

Older and older, each day she grows colder
when she learns her condition is anything but rare.
Realization clicks as her soul begins to molder.

Drowning her dreams in the sand, they start to smolder.
The clinging failure forcefully breathes in the air.
Older and older, each day she grows colder.

A lifetime of regret is perched on each shoulder,
while a world undiscovered waits for her somewhere.
Realization clicks as her soul begins to molder.

Daring to dream, her imagination grows bolder.
Aging was something she was told to beware;
older and older, each day she grows colder.

Over time, her passions have become a simple placeholder
and she convinces herself she never did care.
Realization clicks as her soul begins to molder.

Ignoring her desires has never consoled her,
so, she clings to the last year she has to spare.
Older and older, each day she grows colder,
realization clicks as her soul begins to molder.

Convalescence

"Just one day more"
  he tells himself, as the breath
  he spent days crafting
  evaporates from his mouth.
He's almost there, truly, although his nose
has grazed the finish line for weeks now.

Frustration pools in his chest
like an oil spill itching for a spark.
No sun in months,
his skin has become bloated
from unshed tears.

Dreadfully powerless,
he stays silent
as he waits for fate
to make the next decision.
Suddenly, oxygen escapes his lungs,
deflating the sad sacks.

His eyelids twist shut
like the cap on his medicine bottle.
This will all be over soon,
by the time he counts to three,
he believes; but he is mistaken.
The miracle of reaching the number ten
causes his soul to awaken.

Against all odds, a sliver of warmth
drills through the dusty blinds.
He follows the light
with his eyes and smiles.

Soon after, his hands begin to follow.

Eli's Lingering Embers

I loved that boy
with his hooked nose and dying too soon.
His laugh would always burst out of his body
like the squish of a much too-ripe berry.
He had a deep voice that billowed out in waves of crimson cherry,
and the sharp angles of his bones stretched against his skin;
millimeters away from tasting the outside air.

Fantasies of travel filled his mind
as he gazed playfully at pink treetops.
Something tells me he would have liked Tokyo bubblegum.
Maybe I'm wrong, but there was a certain sweetness
to being his orange peeler: someone he needed.
The oranges I've come across since then
are stickered with "Florida" and his ghostly grip.

Once upon a time, conspiracies raged without restraint
behind the black blaze of eyes that could not be seen.
There was no need for him to showboat,
he soaked up attention hiding in the shadows of the day.
His warnings laced with prayers and desperation terrified me.
His words were like dense pieces of stone
wrapped in barbed wire, wounding me at every turn.
My heart has never recovered from loving that burn of a boy.

Ghost Man Blues

His eyes are two glass marbles
clouded with age and doubt.
The thick film guards from intruders
nosing their way to the truth.

The tip of his tongue is sour,
weighed down by loss,
as it lies within the ravine
found between his teeth.

Failure and disappointment
from the task of living,
have bypassed the grease trap of his soul.
The resulting misery has clogged his arteries.

Nothing ever sits right within his chest.
Throughout the night, his thoughts
burn a hole through his heart
and he just calls it indigestion.

When he believes no one is listening,
he whistles into the silent embrace of the wind,
which reflects the tune back—
in a nearly empty perfection.

Origami Horse

He watches her carefully crafted paper form
soar above the rooftops. Unrestrained,
curiosity fuels her flight. Purity is etched
into her heart, like a fire-licked scar from branding.

She smells like mountaintops and riverbeds.
Her voice is the sound of a captivating applause,
engrossing every nerve in his body.

Flowers bloom on the surface of her retinas. Hazy
sunshine is reflected through her corneas. A kaleidoscope
of unprecedented blessings. Dumbfoundingly divine.

Sage and evergreen are cloaked within her
enthusiastic fervor. Tenderness shyly plays
peek-a-boo within the exciting energy she emits.

Simple Connemara beauty triggers an insatiable need
to defy gravity. Stretching his shoulder out of its socket,
the promise of salvation awaits within the fibers of her mane.

Desperation taints his bones, paralysis looming
as he reaches for the frail fragment of innocence
presented to him. Weightless, the ivory stallion retreats.

Self-inflicted silence has stripped his soul bare.
No identity. No direction. Panic grips his ankles
as he realizes he has forgotten how to fly.

Dread ensnares his mind as understanding sinks in.
An ethereal creature is impossible to capture, and
touching the tip of her tail would baptize him indefinitely.

Determination surges through his chest as
vulnerability escapes his control, like spiders
fleeing to villages hidden in the cracks of walls.

The grip around his ankles loosens, as wings sprout
simultaneously from either side of his spine.
Authenticity shines from his core like freshly polished silver.

Gazing toward the sky, he weeps, when finally,
the origami horse silently offers him her muzzle.

About the Author

Yvonne Beaudry is not the best multitasker. Nobody can count the number of times that she was forced to put down a dish mid-wash—just to write down a few lines that might be used in a poem. After over a decade of writing poetry, she is finally releasing a poetry collection into the world. Freewriting, music, and video games are some of her best tools for striking up inspiration.

For more information visit beaudrypoetry.com or check out 'beaudrypoetry' on social media (Facebook and Instagram).

www.ingramcontent.com/pod-product-compliance
Lightning Source LLC
Chambersburg PA
CBHW060355050426
42449CB00011B/2995